HOW TO BE A HERO

With most books, you read from the beginning to the end and then stop. You can then read it backwards if you like, but that would be silly.

But in this book, you're the hero. That's why it's called *I Hero*, see?

You read a bit, then you make a choice that takes you to a different part of the book. You might jump from Section 3 to Section 47 or Section 28. Crazy, huh?

If you make a good choice, **GREAT!**

BUUUUUUT...

If you make the wrong choice, **ALL KINDS OF BAD STUFF WILL HAPPEN.**

Hah-ha! Loser! You'll have to start again.

But that won't happen to you, will it?
Because you're not a zero — **YOU'RE A HERO!**

You live in a small town. Your ma and pa grow vegetables for your rabbit friends and neighbours. So does everyone else you know.

Ma and Pa want you to help them run the farm, but you would rather invent stuff like this *AMAZING* super-fast-freeze ray gun.

You've come into town in the pick-up to help your ma and pa sell their crop at the market.

"Put that there gun contraption down!" grumbles Pa. "There ain't never gonna be no call for your dumb inventions!"

"But I thought we could *FREEZE* our vegetables..." you protest.

"Hogwash!" says Pa. "Help me stack these here carrots."

Go to 1.

You look closely at the carrots as you stack them on the market stall.

"These carrots look weird," you say. "They're too big — and should they be glowing like this?"

"Aww, shucks. Ain't nothing wrong with them carrots," says Pa. "I picked 'em up cheap at Bad Seed Inc. They're gonna make our fortune!"

Your friend Benny Bunny strolls up. "Hey, great-looking carrots! Can I taste one?"

> **If you want to let Benny try a carrot, go to 23.**
> **If you're not sure about the carrots, go to 12.**

2

You put a cinema staff baseball cap on your head and pin on an employee's badge. As soon as the zombies shamble in, you stop them. "This film is PG rated," you tell them. "I need to see proof of your age."

The zombie bunnies grunt and start looking in their pockets for some ID.

Go to 10.

You lead the zombies into the football stadium.

You look up at the commentator's box, and are surprised to see your pa standing there! He waves at you with a microphone in his hand. While you were rounding up the zombies, he got here first.

Other townsfolk creep up behind the zombies and close all the gates.

You wave at Pa, and the national anthem blares out from the speakers. The zombies look around, confused. Pa panics, presses a few buttons on the sound desk, and finally *"Let it Grow"* plays from every loudspeaker in the stadium! Carrots collapse and zombies freak out!

By the end of the song, the carrots lie still and the rabbits have been

UNZOMBIFIED!

Benny slaps you on the back. "It's over! You're a genius!"

If you agree with Benny, go to 13.

If you think he's making a mistake, go to 39.

4

You and Ma and Pa grab the carrots and try to stuff them back into their sacks.

The carrots might be small, but they're strong, and too quick. Within seconds, they are swarming all over you! Their bites turn your brain to carrot juice.

You've been **ZOMBIFIED!**

Go back to 1.

5

You hand the loud-hailer to Benny, and head for the school, looking for anything that might help you get the kids out. A fire engine with a turntable ladder is parked nearby. In a corner of the schoolyard is a bouncy castle.

If you want to use the fire engine, go to 34.
To use the bouncy castle, go to 22.

6

"Great pickled parsnips!" you cry. "I knew there was something wrong with that carrot! Look what it's done to Benny! It's turned him into a **ZOMBIE BUNNY!**"

The zombie Benny bunny lurches towards you, making terrible grunting noises.

To try and talk to Benny, go to 17.
If you'd rather run away, go to 29.

7

"I think the zombies are scared of the song — to be honest, it scares me a bit too!"

You leave your phone playing "*Let it Grow*" through the cinema's sound system, to keep the zombies away. Benny also has the track, so you borrow his phone.

You sneak up on a shambling zombie bunny, stick headphones into its ears, and play the song. The zombie screams, writhes and goes floppy. When the bunny picks herself up again she has changed back — no more zombie bunny!

"What happened?" she asks.

"It's a long story, but you're cured! The song

is the key!" you say. "Okay, here's the plan..."

If you want to attack the zombies one by one, go to 45.

If you want to move quickly and deal with them all together, go to 28.

8

You look up and see a control booth overlooking the factory floor. There are speakers in the factory for making staff announcements. They must be controlled from there! If you can just reach the sound system and plug your phone into it...

But there are dozens of zombies and hordes of vicious veg between you and the booth!

If you want to attack the vegetables and zombies, go to 47.

If you want to take time to think, go to 36.

9

You run to the stall and lift the protective screen. You pick up a tub of ice cream and dump it over Benny's head.

Benny blinks. "Hey! What's this?"

You check the label. "Chocolate fudge ripple," you say. "Are you okay?"

Benny laughs. "Okay? Me, okay? Sure! Why wouldn't I be okay?"

You shake your head. "Whatever happened to you, the ice cream must've fixed it. Maybe it was the flavour — or it could be because it's cold…"

You are interrupted as your ma and pa come running round the corner — followed by a dozen shambling zombie bunnies!

"They're all over town!" gasps Pa. "What can we do?"

If you want to fight the zombies, go to 16.
If you want to run away, go to 25.

Just then, water rains down from the ceiling. Someone has activated the fire protection sprinkler system.

At the same moment, Pa gets the sound system working. It plays the latest hit from Elsie Eggplant and the Farmhands:

> "Let it grow, let it grow,
> Don't fertilize it anymore!
> Let it grow, let it grow,
> Then stick it in the cooler and slam the door.
> Frozen veg, and fruit sorbet;
> Let the peas freeze on,
>
> 'Cos greens don't appeal to me anyway."

The soggy zombie bunnies go crazy with fear and lurch away!

If you want to chase the zombies, go to 19.
If you want to think about what just happened, go to 24.

11

You take a bike from the shop. "I'll ride to Spudsville for help!" you cry.

You set off. On the bike, you are too fast for the zombie bunnies. They clutch at you in vain.

But at the edge of town, your way is blocked by a zombie bunny horde! You veer off the road — into deep mud, and big trouble.

The bike will not move. You are still trying to tug it free when the zombies attack. You are

ZOMBIFIED!

Go back to 1.

12

"I'm not sure, Benny. They look weird," you say.

"Awww! Come on!" says Benny. But when you turn your back, he grabs a carrot and bounds away.

"Hey, Benny! Bring that back!" you cry.

Benny pauses at the street corner and dangles the carrot. "Come and get it!"

Go to 33.

13

You accept the congratulations of the townsfolk and go home with Ma and Pa.

But that night, you hear creaking and groaning noises all over the house. You open your eyes and turn on the light.

Your bedroom is full of bloodthirsty carrots and zombie bunnies.

"It's just a nightmare, right?" you squeak.

WRONG!

Slavering carrots and bunnies pounce.

You are **ZOMBIFIED!**

Go back to 1.

The cinema is showing the latest zombie movie: Bunnyland, rated PG. You look inside the building — there are no zombies.

"Make sure they can't get in through the fire exits," you tell Ma and Pa. "Benny and I will go out and round up survivors."

"But how do we let everyone know where to come?" asks Benny as you leave the cinema.

If you decide to use a loud-hailer, go to 27.

If you think it would be better to try the radio station, go to 41.

15

You break into the factory and set the air-con to SUPER CHILL MODE.

But the zombies and vegetables spot you and close in. Too late, you realise that the air-con will take a long time — maybe hours — to make the temperature low enough.

That's too slow for you! You are swamped by monstrous mindless mutations and **ZOMBIFIED!**

Go back to 1.

16

"Grab the ice cream!" you cry.

You dump ice cream tubs on the leading zombies. Benny helps you. But you soon run out of tubs, and the remaining zombies grab you before you can run!

The zombies' bites send you straight to la-la land. You've been

Go back to 1.

17

"Benny!" you cry. "It's me! Your old pal!"

But Benny doesn't hear you. He doesn't recognise you! He reaches out with grasping paws, and plunges his great big bucky teeth into your neck!

You feel like you've just swallowed a whole bowl of hot spicy carrot soup all in one go. Then your mind drains away like bathwater.

You've been…

Go back to 1.

18

You burst into the radio studio and grab the microphone. "Hey, everyone!" you cry, "get to the cinema, it's the only safe place in— *blub… burble… bibble…*"

The reason you say this is that the zombie DJ has just bitten your hand holding the microphone. Tough luck — you've been

ZOMBIFIED!

Go back to 1.

19

You chase the zombies as they shamble away.

But when they are a block away from the cinema, they calm down and shuffle round before heading back towards you.

You skid to a halt and turn to run, but too late! Zombie paws clutch at you and bunny teeth bite down.

You've been **ZOMBIFIED!**

Go back to 1.

20

You race to the stall and grab whatever sports equipment you can. You hurl golf balls, baseball bats and hockey sticks at Benny. They bounce off. You pick up a racket and smash tennis balls at him. They don't even slow him down.

Before you can think of anything else, you are in the grip of zombie Benny. His long teeth chomp into your shoulder. Instantly, you lose the plot. You've been **Z-O-M-B-I-F-I-E-D!**

Go back to 1.

21

You play "*Let it Grow*" on your phone, and burst into the factory. Inside there is too much noise from the machinery processing the vegetables, and the zombie slaves can't hear the song. The zombie workers turn to face you. They smell fresh meat!

If you want to attack the zombies, go to 47.

If you want to try and find a way to boost the song volume, go to 8.

22

You run to the bouncy castle and drag it towards the school, knocking zombie bunnies out of the way as you go.

"Jump!" you call.

One by one, the kids jump onto the bouncy castle and bounce over the fence, escaping the zombies. As soon as they are all safe, you lead them to the cinema.

Go to 37.

"Sure," you say.

Benny takes one bite of the carrot — and gasps! He chokes. He crosses his eyes and clutches his throat!

He goes "**OOOH!**" and "**AARGH!**" and "**YAGGAYAGGAYAGGAYEURCH!**" and smoke comes out of his ears!

When the smoke clears, you realise that something terrible has happened to Benny!

Go to 6.

24

Ma, Pa and Benny join you in the entrance. "Sorry about the sprinklers," says Pa. "Must've mixed them up with the volume control."

You aren't listening. "Let's figure this out," you say. "A zombie virus or something has mutated the carrots. Then the rabbits eat the carrots and become zombie bunnies. But why did they run just now?"

If you think the zombies were scared by the water, go to 32.

If you think the zombies were scared by the song, go to 7.

25

You run with Ma, Pa and Benny. As soon as you have escaped the nearest zombie bunnies, you stop between a bicycle shop and your market stall.

Your eyes pop out of your head! On your stall, carrots are moving! They're growing stumpy legs, stubby arms — and drooling mouths with gnashing teeth!

You gaze at them in horror. "We need a plan," you say.

If you want to destroy the carrots, go to 4.

If you would rather take a bike and ride for help, go to 11.

If you decide to escape in Ma and Pa's pick-up truck, go to 35.

26

You run to the pick-up truck and grab the gun from where Pa made you dump it that morning.

You check it over. It looks okay. All you have to do is find somewhere to plug it in, wait a couple of minutes for it to charge, and — **ZAMMO!**

You look over at the factory. Should you make a frontal assault through the main doors, or try and sneak in via the roof?

If you want to use the main doors, go to 42.

If you want to sneak in, go to 31.

You find a loud-hailer in the cinema manager's office.

A few minutes later, you are back in the pick-up. You use the loud-hailer to tell survivors of the zombie plague to head for the cinema.

Benny drives past the local school. The playground is full of zombie bunnies. The kids are trapped on the first floor, calling for help.

You groan. "Those kids need help — but we have to pass on the message to get everyone to the cinema before the zombies get them!"

If you decide to help the kids, go to 5.
If you think getting other survivors to safety is more important, go to 43.

28

Half an hour later, you lead a company of courageous cavies down the main street of the town. You are all carrying mobile phones playing "Let it Grow".

Zombies shamble behind you. Carrots run between their shambling feet. They all want to bite you, but the song keeps them at a distance.

"It's working!" says Benny. "Where do we lead them?"

If you want to lead the zombies out of town, go to 49.

If you decide to lead them to the football stadium, go to 3.

29

Zombie Benny bunny lurches towards you. You run down the street and turn a corner.

To your left is a coffee shop with very few customers.

To your right are more market stalls.

To hide in the coffee shop, go to 38.

If you want to duck down behind a market stall, go to 44.

30

When you get to your farm, Benny helps you and Ma and Pa close the shutters and lock the doors. You move furniture to barricade every way in or out.

But you have barely finished before the zombie bunnies arrive in force! They smash down your flimsy barricades. There is nowhere to run, nowhere to hide. You are *ZOMBIFIED!*

Go back to 1.

31

You climb the fire escape to the roof and get in through an open skylight.

You are on a gantry above the factory floor. You plug your ray gun into a nearby socket. It whines at it charges. After a couple of minutes, a green light glows. Ready!

You point the ray gun down and fire. Its beams sweep over zombies and veg. Where the beam touches, zombies freeze — blink — and return to normal bunnies. Vegetables shudder and lie still.

Minutes later the factory is full of bewildered bunnies and harmless fruit and veg. The attack of the zombie bunnies is over!

Go to 50.

32

You snatch a couple of water-filled fire extinguishers from the entrance, and rush out to spray two nearby zombie bunnies. The zombies look puzzled (and wet), but the water seems to have no other effect.

"It must be the song that scares them," you say, as you race back to the cinema.

Go to 7.

33

Benny disappears around the corner, and shortly afterwards you hear a terrible racket from around the corner — screams and horrible gristly noises and lots of smoke.

Then you hear yells of terror. Panicking townsfolk run around the corner. And lurching after them comes... *THIS!*

Go to 6.

You decide to use the fire engine ladder
to rescue the kids.

You climb into the cab and try to swing the
ladder towards the school. But the controls are
very complicated! The ladder shoots out and
spears a giant hot-dog sign from the roof of a
drive-through restaurant.

The commotion attracts the zombie
bunnies, who drag you screaming
from the cab. You've been

ZOMBIFIED!

Go back to 1.

You manage to dodge the zombies and get to the
pick-up truck. You climb aboard and Pa starts the
engine. You take off in a cloud of dust.

But where should you go now?

To go back to your farm, go to 30.

**If you want to find somewhere you can
hold out against the zombies, go to 46.**

36

You think hard.

What if it's not the song itself that terrifies the zombies — what if it's something in the words?

The song is about freezing fruit and veg...

"That's it!" you cry. "Cold! Cold destroys the mutation! That's why the ice cream worked on Benny!"

But, should you set the factory air-conditioning to low, and chill your foes that way? Or should you use your EXPERIMENTAL and UNTRIED super-fast-freeze ray gun that Pa says will NEVER BE ANY GOOD TO ANYONE?

To use the air-con, go to 15.

To use the freeze-gun, go to 26.

37

The cinema is now packed with terrified townsfolk.

"I reckon I've got the sound system working," Pa tells you. "I'll put some music on to cheer folk up, as soon as I can connect it to this here new-fangled smartphone..."

Ma runs in. "There are zombie bunnies all

around the cinema! And blood-sucking carrots! They're gonna break in…"

If you want to fight the zombie bunnies, go to 48.

If you want to try to trick them, go to 2.

38

You go into the coffee shop and try to hide.

The hamster behind the counter calls, "You want a coffee?"

But then, zombie Benny shambles in. The shop worker screams and runs.

You head to the back of the shop — but there's only one door out, and it's locked!

You're still wrestling with the door handle when you feel Benny's zombie teeth plunge into your shoulder and your brain turns to mush. Oh, dear. You've been

ZOMBIFIED!

Go back to 1.

You leave the townsfolk to celebrate. They've been through enough today. But you know the contaminated carrots came from Bad Seed Inc, and you have to make sure there aren't any more.

It's getting dark as you take the pick-up truck and drive to the Bad Seed processing factory. Looking through a window confirms your worst fears! The building is seething with mutated fruit and veg: brutal broccoli, lethal leeks, killer

cucumbers, savage sweetcorn and murderous melons, all tended by mindless zombie bunny slaves!

If you want to attack the vegetables and zombies, go to 47.

If you want to defeat them with "Let it Grow" played on your phone, go to 21.

If you want to play the song another way, go to 8.

40

You pull up outside the stadium and go in.

But there are already zombies on the field. You realise the stadium has far too many entrances and exits to keep them out.

"This is no good," you say.

If you want to go back to your farm, go to 30.

If you would rather try the cinema, go to 14.

41

You head for the radio studios of FARM FM.

You enter the control room, and see to your

horror that the rabbit DJ is muttering gibberish and putting on tracks at random.

"Holy horseradish!" you say. "He's a **MINDLESS ZOMBIE!**"

"I listen to his show," says Benny. "He's always like that."

If you want to change your mind and use the loud-hailer, go to 27.

If you still want to send a message over the radio, go to 18.

You burst in through the doors. Quickly, you plug in the ray gun. It whines as it starts to charge.

You laugh. "Cool!" You point the gun and pull the trigger.

Nothing happens. You shake the gun. "Er..."

Too late you remember that the gun takes two minutes to charge — and you haven't got two minutes.

The factory echoes to your shrieks as you are

Z-O-M-B-I-F-I-E-D!

Go back to 1.

43

"We should help those kids," says Benny.

"We'd never get past the zombies," you say. "Keep going."

Suddenly, the truck's engine dies. As Benny desperately tries to restart it, zombie bunnies surround the truck and drag you to your doom.

DOH! You've been ZOMBIFIED!

Go back to 1.

44

You duck behind the market stalls. For a while, nothing happens. You look up — and find yourself staring into the leering face of zombie Benny! He's found you!

You look around desperately for something you can use to defend yourself.

If you want to grab something from a sporting goods stall, go to 20.

If you would rather head for an ice-cream stall, go to 9.

45

You and Benny stalk zombie bunnies with your headphones playing "Let it Grow". You clamp headsets over zombie bunny ears.

But the song takes time to work on the

zombies. As you are playing the track to the third shuddering zombie, you feel a terrible pain in your arm. Another zombie has crept up on you — you've been

ZOMBIFIED!

Go back to 1.

46

You drive around town looking for places where your fellow infection-free townsfolk can gather in safety from zombie bunnies and mutated carrots. You need somewhere big that is also easy to defend.

To try the football stadium, go to 40.
If you would rather try the cinema, go to 14.

47

Howling a ninja guinea-pig challenge, you leap forward to attack.

At first, your razor-sharp vegetable knives and peelers wreak havoc! Carrot-peelings litter the floor and tomato juice is splashed all over the walls.

But the vile vegetables fight back. Their zombie slaves soon overpower you.

In seconds, the fighting is over and you are

ZOMBIFIED!

Go back to 1.

48

You go down to the entrance "We're going to fight our way out!" you cry.

Some of the younger guinea pigs, hamsters and mice arm themselves with ice-cream tubs from the cold store.

You all rush out, hurling pint-sized pots of ice cream. But they are too small to stop the zombies. Within seconds, your tiny animal force is overwhelmed!

You've been **ZOMBIFIED!**

Go to 1.

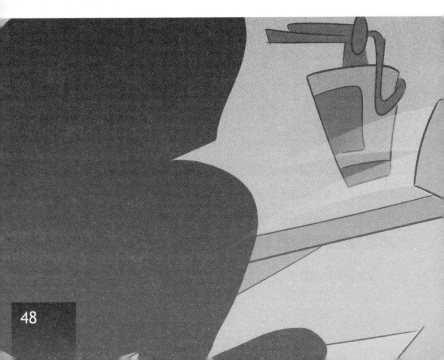

49

You lead the zombie bunnies out of town.
You want to get them as far away as possible.

But one by one, the phone batteries start
to die. As they do so, the zombies close in.

Eventually, only one phone is playing.
"*Let it...*"

Silence.

The zombies pounce. You are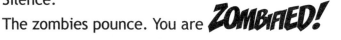

Go back to 1.

50

The townsfolk are still celebrating as you return.

Pa slaps you on the back. "I'm proud of you!
I never thought I'd be glad you got yourself a
college eddication." He takes a bite out of a
carrot. Seeing your expression, he laughs. "Don't
worry. These here veg are harmless now. We've
been eatin' them all evening." He sighs. "Mind
you, I reckon I've had my fill of carrots for a

while. I think I'll get into potatoes. I got some of those from Bad Seed Inc, too." He drops a potato into your paws. "What do you think of that?"

You stare at the potato. "It's got eyes."

Pa shrugs. "All potatoes have eyes."

"Yes, but these eyes are open! And it's **_LOOKING_** at me!!!..."

You are a kitten living in a tough, rough part of the city. The streets are ruled by the Ugly Pug gang. They take what they want, when they want and don't let anyone get in their way. They rule by fear.

You and the other cats and creatures of the city have never stood up to them. But maybe it's about time that someone did...

You are walking along the street minding your own business. Turning a corner, you see a group of Ugly Pug gang members robbing an old female, ginger cat.

She sees you and cries out, "Help me!"

If you want to help, go to 24.
If you want to ignore her, go to 28.

Continue the adventure in:

About the 2Steves

"The 2Steves" are
Britain's most popular
writing double act
for young people,
specialising in comedy
and adventure. They
perform regularly in schools and libraries,
and at festivals, taking the power of words
and story to audiences of all ages.

Together they have written many books,
including the *I HERO Immortals* and *iHorror* series.

About the illustrator: Lee Robinson

Lee studied animation at Newcastle College and
went on to work on comics such as *Kung Fu
Panda* as well as running comicbook workshops
throughtout the northeast of England. When he's not
drawing, Lee loves running, reading and videogames.
He now lives in Edmonton, Canada, where's he's got
plenty of time to come up with crazy ideas while
waiting for the weather to warm up.

I HERO Legends — collect them all!

ATHENA

978 1 4451 5234 9 pb
978 1 4451 5235 6 ebook

BEOWULF

978 1 4451 5225 7 pb
978 1 4451 5226 4 ebook

KING ARTHUR

978 1 4451 5231 8 pb
978 1 4451 5232 5 ebook

FREYA

978 1 4451 5237 0 pb
978 1 4451 5238 7 ebook

HERCULES

978 1 4451 5228 8 pb
978 1 4451 5229 5 ebook

ROBIN HOOD

978 1 4451 5183 0 pb
978 1 4451 5184 7 ebook

Have you read the I HERO Atlantis Quest mini series?

MENACE FROM THE DEEP

978 1 4451 2867 2 pb
978 1 4451 2868 9 ebook

OCEAN ALLIANCE

978 1 4451 2870 2 pb
978 1 4451 2871 9 ebook

BATTLE FOR THE SEAS

978 1 4451 2876 4 pb
978 1 4451 2877 1 ebook

ATLANTIS ASSAULT

978 1 4451 2873 3 pb
978 1 4451 2874 0 ebook

Also by the 2Steves...

978 1 445 5104 5 pb
978 1 445 5119 9 eBook

You are a skilled, stealthy ninja. Your village has been attacked by a warlord called Raiden. Now YOU must go to his castle and stop him before he destroys more lives.

978 1 445 5101 4 pb
978 1 445 5117 5 eBook

You are the Warrior Princess. Someone wants to steal the magical ice diamonds from the Crystal Caverns. YOU must discover who it is and save your kingdom.

978 1 445 5103 8 pb
978 1 445 5121 2 eBook

You are a magical unicorn. Empress Yin Yang has stolen Carmine, the red unicorn. Yin Yang wants to destroy the colourful Rainbow Land. YOU must stop her!

978 1 445 5102 1 pb
978 1 445 5124 3 eBook

You are a spy, codenamed Scorpio. Someone has taken control of secret satellite laser weapons. YOU must find out who is responsible and stop their dastardly plans.